STEM JOBS WITH
Animals

Shirley Duke

rourkeeducationalmedia.com

Scan for Related Titles and Teacher Resources

Before Reading:

Building Academic Vocabulary and Background Knowledge

Before reading a book, it is important to tap into what your child or students already know about the topic. This will help them develop their vocabulary, increase their reading comprehension, and make connections across the curriculum.

1. Look at the cover of the book. What will this book be about?
2. What do you already know about the topic?
3. Let's study the Table of Contents. What will you learn about in the book's chapters?
4. What would you like to learn about this topic? Do you think you might learn about it from this book? Why or why not?
5. Use a reading journal to write about your knowledge of this topic. Record what you already know about the topic and what you hope to learn about the topic.
6. Read the book.
7. In your reading journal, record what you learned about the topic and your response to the book.
8. After reading the book complete the activities below.

Content Area Vocabulary
Read the list. What do these words mean?

client
competitive
data
design
enrichment
expert
infect
poultry
precise
specialize
veterinarian

After Reading:

Comprehension and Extension Activity

After reading the book, work on the following questions with your child or students in order to check their level of reading comprehension and content mastery.

1. Describe the role of STEM in working with animals. (Summarize)
2. Why is technology important in the farming industry? (Infer)
3. How similar is your doctor's job to a veterinarian's? (Text to self connection)
4. What role does data play in learning about wildlife populations? (Summarize)
5. Describe how a bird's cage might be different from a hamster's cage. (Visualize)

Extension Activity

After reading this book, consider the ways in which STEM fields may be helpful in protecting endangered species. Write a persuasive essay encouraging those interested in animals to study science, technology, engineering, and mathematics.

nts

What Is STEM?

A zookeeper prepares lunch for an elephant. A **veterinarian** gives a puppy his shots. An engineer designs a new type of chicken coop.

These jobs all seem different, but they all began with a STEM subject. STEM is a short way to talk about the fields of science, technology, engineering, and mathematics.

STEM jobs are careers for the future. STEM jobs meet needs people have. They will supply answers to questions we haven't even thought of yet. A STEM education could prepare you to find the next great discovery!

What's STEM?

Science
Technology
Engineering
Mathematics

Do Feed the Animals

Visiting a zoo can be fun, but more goes on at the zoo than simply looking at animals. Before visitors arrive a flurry of action takes place. The director readies paperwork. Ticket sellers set up their booths before people arrive. The kitchen is busy preparing food for the animals.

Zoos house animals from all over the world. They care for penguins, elephants, tarantulas, and lions, just to name a few. The zoo nutritionist knows exactly what the animals need to stay healthy. Zoo nutritionists make sure the animals get the right amount of nutrients to match their natural diet.

STEM in Action!

Look at two or more pet food ingredient labels. If you don't have any pets, visit the pet store and look at the pet food labels there.

Read the ingredient labels of dry dog food and dry cat food. The first item listed is the ingredient present in the highest amount in the food. What is the first item listed for dog and cat food? How do the number of ingredients compare?

Now compare dry dog food with wet, canned dog food. What differences do you see on these labels?

Compare food labels for different animals, like dogs, cats, fish, and gerbils. How do the ingredients compare?

In the wild, elephants eat grass, fruit, leaves, and bark. They eat between 165 and 330 pounds (75 to 150 kilograms) daily. They spend 16 hours per day finding and eating food.

Zoo elephants need less food because they don't have to work to find it. Each elephant eats about 125 pounds (57 kilograms) in one day. An elephant keeper makes sure the elephants are eating enough calories to stay healthy.

Real STEM Job: *Elephant Keeper*

This job includes training and bathing these large mammals. Elephants can be up to 13 feet (3.9 meters) tall! Keepers clean feet, file nails, bring feed, and weigh them.

STEM Fast Fact: Elephants are part of a group called pachyderms. The group includes other thick-skinned mammals like hippos and rhinos.

Elephant keepers also exercise them and provide **enrichment** and play. This includes hiding treats and special training to keep these intelligent mammals busy.

Elephant keepers must be comfortable working with large animals. The job requires a background in biology or zoology to succeed in this **competitive** field. Keepers need good math skills and an ability to communicate well. A positive attitude is also helpful. So is a realistic idea of the work and danger that goes with it.

Pet Gear

All pets need love. More importantly, they need the right food and grooming. Pet groomers use tools like brushes, nail trimmers, and bathing tubs. Pet shampoos are made especially for animals. Ear care may require medication and tools to apply it. Special clippers must be used to trim fur.

Grooming requires a variety of tools. It is important to use the right tool for the job. Engineers **design** products to fit different pets' needs. Bristle brushes work on most pets. Long hair requires wire brushes. Pet shampoos are designed to protect soft skin and prevent drying.

STEM in Action!

What makes a good brush?

Find all the brushes and combs in your home. Gather hairbrushes, toothbrushes, paintbrushes, and any other brushes you can think of.

Now, test each of the brushes on your hair. Rank each brush from best to worst for brushing hair. Look at the design of each of the brushes. Figure out why some brushes are better than others. Which brush was the best? What about its design made it the best for your hair?

Cages, toys, litter boxes, leashes, and more are all designed especially for the pets that will use them. Pet owners have a lot of choices. If one product did not work well for their pet, they can likely find another that will do the job.

Real STEM Job: *Product Engineer*

Pet supply companies are always building new tools to make pet care easier. It is the job of product engineers to develop the tools that pet owners need. They ask pet owners what problems they have caring for their pets. They look at how the pets behave. They look at old products and how they could be improved. Then they use this information to build something better.

For example, product engineers worked to make new and easy ways to clear cat litter. Now, cat owners may use special hi-tech litter boxes. The robotic devices clear dirty litter automatically.

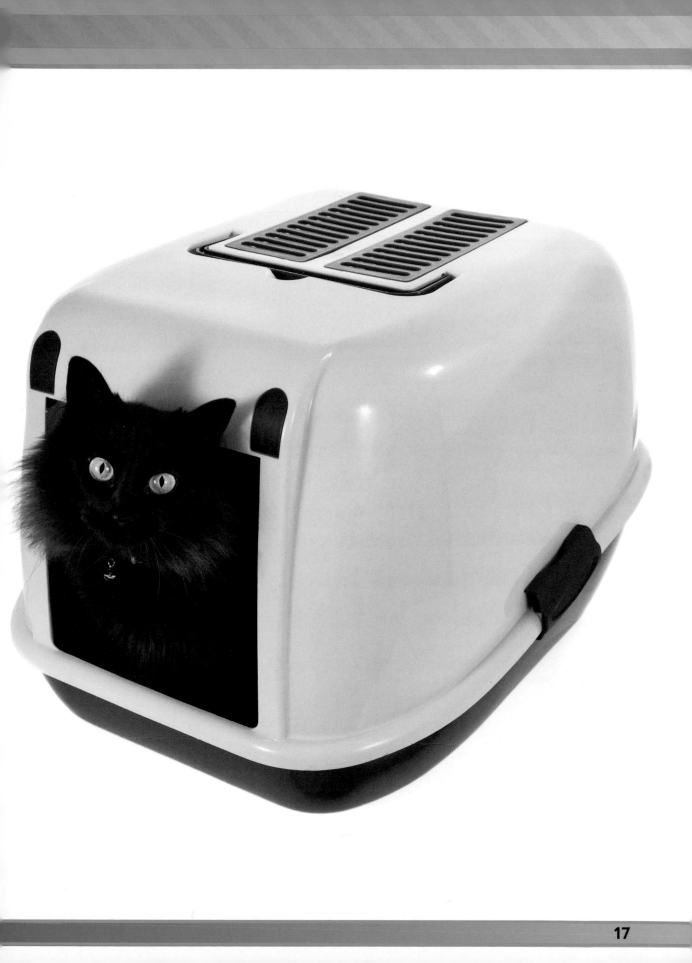

On the Farm

Many people who work with animals do so on farms. Farmers must have **expert** knowledge about the animals they raise.

Farming in the United States is big business. In the United States, more than 51,000 dairy farms produce milk that can be used to make cheese, butter, ice cream, and yogurt. Families own almost 97 percent of these farms. About 75 percent of the farms have fewer than 100 cows. Large dairy farms produce the biggest percentage of milk, almost 85 percent.

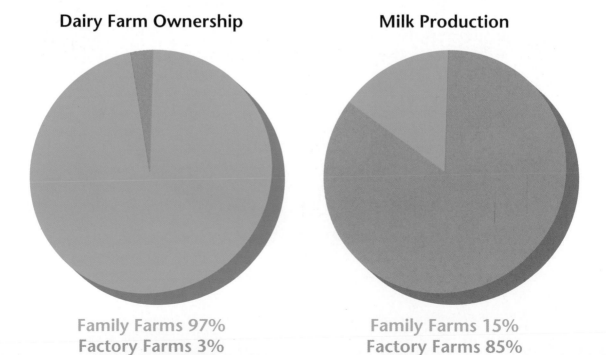

Dairy Farm Ownership

Family Farms 97%
Factory Farms 3%

Milk Production

Family Farms 15%
Factory Farms 85%

In addition to caring for animals, farmers must have strong business skills. They monitor how much milk their cows are producing and plan for the future. If their cows are not making enough milk to cover the cost of caring for the farm, the farmer will need to make changes to his or her business.

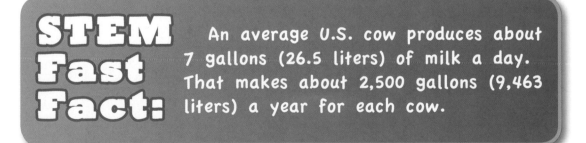

STEM Fast Fact: An average U.S. cow produces about 7 gallons (26.5 liters) of milk a day. That makes about 2,500 gallons (9,463 liters) a year for each cow.

STEM in Action!

If a dairy farm has 75 dairy cattle and each cow produces 7 gallons a day, what is the total amount of milk produced each day on that farm?

$$75 \times 7 = 525$$

The farm produces 525 gallons each day.

Take it further. How many gallons would the farm produce each year? What would happen to the farm's milk production if they sold 5 cows?

Cows must be milked on a dairy farm of any size. Technology today makes machine milking easier than hand milking. Big farms often use a milking parlor. Milking parlors bring the udders closer to a comfortable level for the milkers.

Milk can go bad if it is not kept cool and treated to remove harmful bacteria. The process of heating food to remove bacteria is called pasteurization. Raw milk goes to processors. There, it is heated to a **precise** temperature and prepared to ship across the country. The products are unloaded at stores and sold.

Real STEM Job: *Dairy Farmers*

Dairy farmers manage their cows so that they produce as much milk as possible. To do this, dairy farmers need to understand how cows produce milk. They need to know the best conditions under which to keep their cows.

Cows produce milk after giving birth to a calf. To keep the cow producing milk, the farmer must milk the cow several times each day. However, if the farmer is unable to milk his cows, they will stop making more milk.

The best quality milk requires that cows get a well-balanced diet. Farmers make sure they are eating grasses and clover. They also make sure the cows get enough water. Cows eat about 154 pounds (70 kilograms) of grass and drink about 18 gallons (70 liters) of water per day. The farmers also feed the cows special vitamins and treat them for illnesses.

Designing for Animals

Large **poultry** farms want the latest in energy-saving chicken coops to house their growing flocks. The chickens need protection from too much heat or cold. They must have a safe place to rest at night. The poultry workers have to feed large numbers of birds at one time. Insect control is a problem.

Chickens that will become food have been bred to produce more meat. They are affected by heat, dust, and waste. A large coop has to be designed to fit the chickens' needs. It must also save money and energy. An agricultural engineer listens to what the company selling the chickens wants and designs equipment to meet those needs.

STEM in Action!

A large chicken gets 4 square feet of space in a coop. If a chicken farmer has a coop that is 8 feet by 36 feet, how many chickens can he raise?

8 feet x 36 feet = 288 square feet

288 square feet ÷ 4 square feet = 72 chickens

The farmer can raise 72 chickens in his coop!

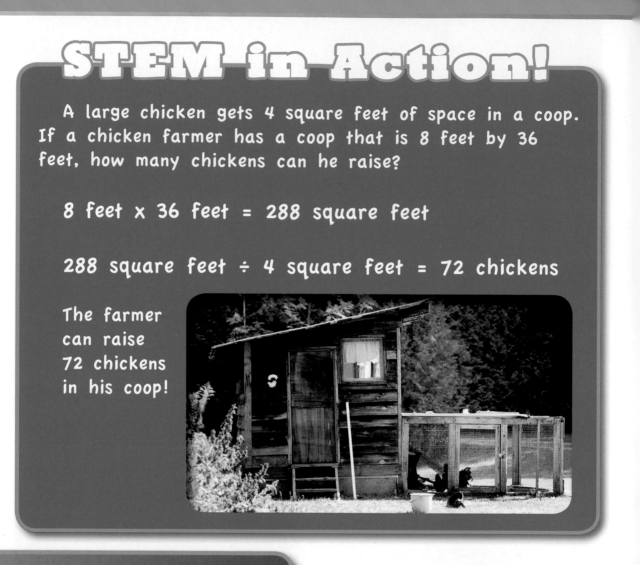

STEM Fast Fact:

An eggshell isn't solid. There are 8,000 tiny holes for air to pass through. Baby chicks breathe inside the eggs before they hatch.

Chicken eggs take 21 days to hatch, but most duck eggs take 28 days.

Agricultural engineers work on many kinds of activities. They may design animal-related products. They may build homes for animals to live in or devices to help farmers collect chicken eggs or milk cows. These devices help both the farmers and the animals.

Real STEM Job: *Agricultural Engineer*

Agricultural engineers who want to work with animals **specialize** in making devices for livestock. If a **client** wants to build a new hen house that fits the growing chickens, the engineer listens to the client's needs and looks for a solution. Agricultural engineers work to keep costs down and make buildings energy efficient. They often use computer-aided design (CAD), which shows the buyers what the final product will look like.

Agricultural engineers may work with many different kinds of animals. From fish, to chickens, to pigs, agricultural engineers design devices that keep the animals' well-being in mind. They help the farmers take care of their livestock, while also keeping the farmers' business moving forward. The more eggs, milk, and meat the farmer can produce, the better his business will do.

Into the Wild

A team of wildlife biologists trek into the woods to check their traps. They have caught an American robin. The biologists carefully place a small band around the robin's leg before they let it fly away.

Lightweight bands are best for tracking small song birds. But some wildlife biologists use GPS and Doppler technology to track larger birds and animals. They get precise **data** about the animals' movements. However, this technology is too heavy for small birds to carry. It is also expensive, so biologists can track fewer animals with this method.

Pacific Ocean

Canada

United States of America

Atlantic Ocean

M

American Robin Migration Area

summer-only range

winter-only range

year-round range

Often, wildlife scientists work in teams. They rely on the information learned by other scientists, who work in ecology or water science. Many wildlife scientists specialize in a group of animals, such as mammals or birds. Others focus on a habitat, like the marine biologists who study saltwater life.

Wildlife biologists conduct research, both inside and outside of a lab setting.

STEM in Action!

Wildlife biologists often keep track of populations of the animals they study. Records for one caribou herd showed a population of 100,000 in the first year and 178,000 in the second year. The third year's population was 123,000. What was the average population over the three years? First, add the three years of population data together.

100,000 + 178,000 + 123,000 = 401,000

The populations over the three years equaled 401,000. To get the average, the total population of 401,000 is divided by 3 years.

401,000 ÷ 3 = 133,667

The average population for three years was 133,667 caribou.

Wildlife biologists track animal populations. They record the numbers on a grid. Then they add up the totals. They may use photographs of the herd to count the number for each grid.

Wildlife biologists sometimes study one small part of an animal's characteristics. Others may look at part of their life cycle or work with them at the cell level. Some focus on the whole community or ecosystem of the population.

Real STEM Job: *Wildlife Biologist*

Wildlife biologists often focus on one thing about that animal. Then they research to find out everything about the animal that has been studied already. Basic research answers questions about how the species functions or evolves. Applied research shows biologists ways to solve problems.

Jane Goodall
1934–

Jane Goodall is famous for her work with chimpanzees in Africa. She spent years in the wild, studying their behaviors.

Wildlife biologists also look at behavior. They see what makes an animal do the things it does. They learn about the animals in their habitat. They explore the animals' place in the ecosystem.

They write about what they learned in science journals. Some teach or present lectures to let others know their findings. Information builds up over years. Each time the animal or species is studied, new information is learned. Many biologists become experts in their field of study.

Pet Medicine

When your family pet is sick, it's time for a trip to the veterinarian. The vet will diagnose what is wrong and work to cure the problem. They may prescribe medicine or a special diet to get your pet feeling better. They also repair broken bones if your pet has been injured.

Vets treat all kinds of animals. In addition to dogs and cats, vets care for birds, rabbits, ferrets, reptiles, and other animals that people keep as pets.

Most veterinarians work in clinics, but some do research, work in food safety, or travel to ranches and farms to work. Some work at zoos. Vets often need to be on hand when animals have their babies. They monitor the mother's health and assist in the delivery if necessary.

STEM in Action!

Imagine you have a broken arm. What would the doctor do to treat it? The doctor would set your bone in a cast. This would make it difficult for you to write, eat, and brush your teeth.

What would happen if a dog or cat broke its leg? How would it get around? Make a guess and then research the answer.

Now, imagine that a bird has broken its wing. Would the treatment be different for this animal? How so?

Did you know that some animal illnesses can **infect** humans? Keeping pets healthy keeps humans healthy, too. Many dogs are vaccinated against diseases like rabies, hepatitis, and lyme disease.

Real STEM Job: *Emergency Medicine Veterinarian*

When there is a medical emergency you go to the emergency room at a nearby hospital. But what if an animal is having an emergency? Then you would take the animal to a vet who specializes in emergency medicine.

When prompt care is needed these vets give life-saving care. They give the animal medicine, perform surgery, and treat dangerous wounds. They will monitor the animal carefully to make sure it is improving.

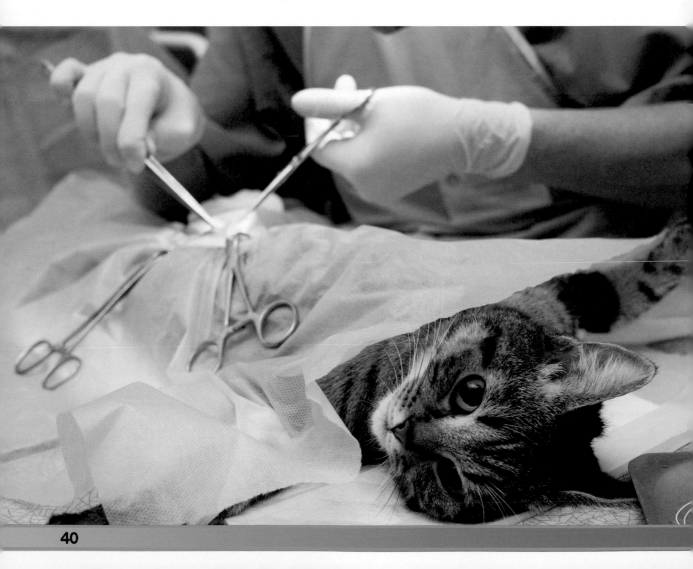

Your regular vet may have the training necessary to care for your pet in an emergency situation. Or you may have to take your pet to a special animal hospital where they have the tools to treat your pet.

When there is a serious emergency, these vets could help save your pet's life!

STEM Jobs with Animals for You

Working with animals is satisfying in many ways. Many different kinds of jobs allow people to find the one that interests them. Animals play a major part in the lives of many people. Animal careers will be around for a long time.

STEM jobs are the jobs for the future. In the future, more and more careers will depend on STEM knowledge. Getting an education is important, but choosing a STEM field with animals helps animals and people while giving you a satisfying career.

STEM Job Fact Sheet

Elephant Keeper

Important Skills: Animal Behavior, Communication, Positive Attitude

Important Knowledge: Biology, Zoology, Mathematics, Science, Elephant Zoology

College Major: Life Science, Zoology

Median Salary: $26,580

Product Engineer

Important Skills: Complex Problem-Solving, Critical Thinking, Mathematics, Reading Comprehension

Important Knowledge: Engineering, Mathematics, Chemistry, Design, Marketing

College Major: Engineering

Median Salary: $61,125

Agricultural Engineer

Important Skills: Attention to Detail, Analytical Thinking, Dependability, Initiative, Persistence

Important Knowledge: Critical Thinking, Listening Skills, Creativity, Mathematics, Design, Problem-Solving

College Major: Agricultural Engineering, Biological Engineering

Median Salary: $71,090

Dairy Farmer

Important Skills: Dairy Farming, Veterinary, Analytical, Critical Thinking, Machine Operations

Important Knowledge: Farm Management, Dairy Science, Economics, Animal Science, Technology

College Major: Dairy Science, Farm Management, Experience

Median Salary: $60,750

Wildlife Biologist

Important Skills: Research, Observation, Critical Thinking, Analysis, Speaking, Writing

Important Knowledge: Science, Technology, Computer, Mathematics, Anatomy, Cell Biology, Chemistry

College Major: Zoology, Biology, Wildlife Biology, Ecology

Median Salary: $57,430

Emergency Medicine Veterinarian

Important Skills: Interpersonal, Problem-Solving, Compassion, Management, Dexterity

Important Knowledge: Biology, Chemistry, Anatomy, Zoology, Animal Science, Microbiology

College Major: Science and Doctor of Veterinary Medicine

Median Salary: $82,040

Glossary

client (KLYE-uhnt): the customer of a company or individual business owner

competitive (kumn-PET-tuh-tiv): a situation where many are trying to win or earn a job or prize

data (DAY-tuh): information that is collected and can be studied

design (di-ZINE): to plan something that can be made

enrichment (en-RICH-muhnt): the addition of something that will improve your life

expert (ek-SPURT): someone who knows a lot about a particular subject

infect (in-FEKT): a germ or disease that is easily spread from one to another

poultry (POHL-tree): farm birds raised from eggs, like chickens, ducks, and turkeys

precise (pri-SISE): very accurate or exact

specialize (SPESH-uh-lize): to focus on one area of work or study

veterinarian (vet-ur-uh-NAIR-ee-uhn): a doctor specially trained to treat and care for sick and injured animals

Index

Show What You Know

1. Identify and write two statements from the book that support the idea of the value of a STEM education.
2. Give two examples from the book of a job that requires working outdoors and explain why they must take place there.
3. Why do product engineers design special brushes for animals?
4. What are two ways that wildlife biologists track animals?
5. How does keeping pets healthy affect human health?

Websites to Visit

www.paws.org/kids-careers-with-animals.html

www.kids.sandiegozoo.org/jobs-zoo

www.jobs.aol.com/articles/2009/01/26/10-jobs-that-let-you-work-with-animals/

About the Author

Shirley Duke has worked in a STEM field most of her life. Her favorite STEM field is science. She taught science in elementary, middle, and high schools before she began writing science books for young people. She enjoys nature and observing its beauty in the Jemez Mountains of New Mexico. She lives part time in New Mexico and Texas with her husband.

Meet The Author!
www.meetREMauthors.com

PHOTO CREDITS: Title Page © dotshock, Jenoche; page 4 © AlexRaths, WoodenDinosaur; page 5 © powerofforever; page 6 © kali9; page 7 © Anan Kaewkhammul; page 8 © Ozgur Ulker, momcilog, alice2072; page 9 © David Tyrer, Tsuji; page 10 © compuinfoto; page 11 © excentric_01, taarnes; page 12 © Jeanne9, cynoclub, zeynepogan; page 13 © JMichl; page 14 © kedsanee, kamkar; page 15 © StockPhotosArt, OKRAD; page 16 © Ulrike Schanz, StockPhotosArt; page 18 © VLIET; page 19 © steverts, scotto72; page 20 © shaunl; page 21 © MiguelMalo; page 22 ©   ; page 23 © Vaida_P; page 24 © My Life Graphic, branislavpudar, terekhov igor; page 25 © Enrico Jose, Christopher Meder; page 26 © hankscorpio, AnthiaCumming; page 27 © Gravicapa, Squaredpixels; page 28 © Lisa-Blue; page 29 © RGtimeline; page 30 © bergserg, crispphotography, Tom Reichner; page 31 © Goodluz, bjmc, LazyTJ; page 32 © Rivendellstudios; page 33 © Stevebrigman; page 34 © anyaivanova; page 35 © Creative Commons, Joanne Zh; page 36 © Fertnig, mwpenny; page 37 © BartCo, DenGuy; page 38 © webphotographeer; page 39 © kali9; page 40 © DimaBerkut; page 41 © CEFutcher; page 42 © MachineHeadz; page 43 © Alexander Raths, Goodluz, branislavpudar

Edited by: Jill Sherman

Cover design by: Renee Brady
Interior design by: Cory Davis

Library of Congress PCN Data

STEM Jobs with Animals/ Shirley Duke
 (STEM Jobs You'll Love)
  ISBN 978-1-62717-698-9 (hard cover)
  ISBN 978-1-62717-820-4 (soft cover)
  ISBN 978-1-62717-934-8 (e-Book)
Library of Congress Control Number: 2014935491

Printed in the United States of America, North Mankato, Minnesota

Also Available as:

Printed in Great Britain
by Amazon

Captain Carson

Bali, Indonesia

May 2019

After all that fun, I think it's time to RELAX.

I really hope that you enjoyed our trip,
and maybe you can visit Indonesia
on your own one day.

See you on our next adventure!

Indonesia is a gorgeous country with so much culture and tradition to experience.

There's even a temple called Goa Gajah, which means "Elephant Cave."

Come on, let's go check it out!

There are several beautiful temples in Bali.

Temples are sacred and peaceful
places for people to pray.

Some temples are in the middle of the ocean,
some are on top of mountains.

In many Asian countries, like Indonesia, you can touch, feed and even take a mud bath with an elephant.

Mud baths help to keep the elephant's skin cool on hot days.

Another animal that is common to see in Bali, is the Elephant.

Let me hear your best elephant sound!

Bali is the home to many animals.

At the Sacred Monkey Forest, there are
"Macaca" monkeys everywhere.

BEWARE!!!

Although they appear to be cute, they are very sneaky
and like to steal your toys, snacks
and even your favorite dinosaur backpack.

or catch some waves on one of Bali's beautiful beaches!

Surf's up dude!

You can soar in the sky like Superman
on the Bali swings,

or see Mount Anung, which is one of Indonesia's active volcanos!

Watch out for Lava!!

There are so many activities that you can do in Bali.

You can pretend to be a baby bird sitting in a nest that overlooks the rice terraces,

It is only 8 degrees south of the equator.

Since it is so close to the equator, it can get really hot here.

Bali is the most visited island in the Indonesian archipelago.

An archipelago is a group of several islands.

Today were going on a trip to Bali.

Make sure to grab your passport, put on your straw hat and let's go on this adventure together.

Hi, my name is Captain Carson, and I love to travel the world.

Traveling introduces you to new people, places and cultures.

Authors Dedication:

This book is dedicated to my

great grandparents,

Virgil and Mary Toombs

Illustrators Dedication:

For Jai & Jaden